Define to Refine Your LIFE

A journey to Refine yourself into the best
and most unique version of your own self

Chaitali Mehta, Premal Parekh

PARTRIDGE

To order additional copies of this book, contact
Partridge India
000 800 10062 62
orders.india@partridgepublishing.com

www.partridgepublishing.com/india

CONTENTS

My Book

This is my first attempt to write what I believe in.
With God's grace, herein I begin my first book.
With the inspiration of my mentor, Mr Premal Parekh, I started writing a book which will help millions of people transform their lives in a positive way.

Chaitali Mehta

Acknowledgements

I am sincerely thankful to all the wonderful people and experiences that helped me discover myself, in this journey of life.

Blessings of the God- Shriji Bawa, my parents, my in-laws and my extended family has been pivotal in writing this book.

The four pillars to whom I owe my success- My husband Paresh, my daughters Kanchi and Khushi and my mentor Mr. Premal Parekh, THANK YOU GUYS for your unconditional love, support and motivation, YOU believed in me before I could.

My virtual gurus who refined me- Sadhguru, B.K Shivani Didi, Gaur Gopal Prabhu, Gyanvatsal Swamiji, Hariswarupdasji Swamiji, Kajal Oza Vaidya and Jim Rohn

I would like to thank my publishing team and some amazing people who tirelessly helped me in editing this book- Thank you dear Simran, Mr. Chetan Shah and Mr. Anil Uchil.

Introduction

Define to Refine Your Life

The simplest and most effective way to success and happiness

Accept no one's definition of your life.
Define yourself.

Robert Frost

It has been observed that people are able to define others, but when it comes to defining themselves, they are unable to do so.

People are always seeking ways to be successful and happy but are rarely able to define what can help them achieve success or make them feel truly happy.

Whatever your life may be today, only you can make a difference to it. We all are like those raw diamonds that are unaware of their shine until they are shaped and *refined*.

So let's begin this journey to refine ourselves into the best and most unique version of our own selves.

The first step to refining yourself is to ask: What is my definition of success? What can truly make me happy?

While seeking our answers, the funny thing is that we often think of what others have told us about their ideas of success and happiness.

For each one of us, the answers would vary, and in fact, they should vary, as we all are different and on different journeys.

Once your desires and dreams are *defined*, you can work on them.

So, my friend, this diary will guide you in *defining* your today and help you set a narrative for your tomorrow.

Remember: *The person you want to be is already within you; otherwise, you would never want to be that person.*

Will it be an easy task? NO.
Will it be worth it? ABSOLUTELY!
The best adventure is to be able to live the life of your dreams.
So say YES to this adventure and unleash your true power.

Why will you love this diary?

1. It will help you focus on your goals, desires, and dreams.
2. A little shift of your focus to the positive side of life can miraculously make you happier.
3. If you begin your day with a positive quote every day and define how you wish to spend your day, it will magically focus all your energy towards making that wish come true.
4. Starting and ending your day by writing in this diary for a few minutes will help you develop a habit of giving up excuses and will make you consistent and focused.
5. Most people may have read a lot about positive thinking but hardly anyone knows how to implement it. This diary will give you nine easy steps to implement all these principles in your daily routine.
6. This diary will contain memorabilia for you, a treasure of your memories, ideas, and dreams.
7. This diary will help you do acts (*weekly challenges*) which you always wanted to do but which you missed somewhere.

8. This diary is designed to be your friend, your mirror, your aide, which will help you *define* and design your today and eventually *refine* your life.

People often wield the excuse of not having *time*.

I truly agree, my friend. We actually don't have time.

The clock is ticking, so before it's too late, we need to live the life we have always desired.

Remember, my friend, it's only when you clearly *define* your wishes, desires, and dreams that you can perceive them, work on them and make them come true.

So let me take you on this journey—*Define to Refine Your Life before You Resign.*

Are you ready for this journey?

Yes, you are!

Your Habits Make You

Aristotle said,
'We are what we repeatedly do. Excellence,
then, is not an act, but a habit.'

How accurate Aristotle was!

This simple principle can actually make or mar our life. A set of repeated actions, just a few acts, if done consciously, can design our personality and the world around us.

We are created by our habits. Our repeated actions *define* our excellence. Excellent sportsmen, excellent actors, excellent doctors, and excellent students are not born... they are created! They are those who have been consistently doing their work every day, without stopping.

Most people believe that a habit means only *repeated actions*. In fact, a habit is more about *repeated thinking*, which creates *repeated actions* and results in the making of a person as he or she is.

Developing a productive habit is challenging but not impossible. You may have experienced that, many a time, you make resolutions like 'I will lose weight' or 'I shall wake up early'.

But you end up breaking them.

Here is the key: *To develop any new habit, one has to perceive that new thought in the right state of mind.*

So when are we in the most receptive mode?

It's the time we wake up afresh. Irrespective of the time of the day, the moment we are back to our consciousness, the ability to think, evaluate, and perceive is at its best.

So we recommend you to keep this diary just next to your bedside with a pen so you can write your first impulse, intuition, and feeling, and set the tone and mood for the rest of your day.

If the day is started with a smile, a creative thought, hope, or a special feeling, then the day should also end with analysing and evaluating it. So just before you go to sleep, spend a few minutes writing what happened if it was really nice, and if it was a bad day, then you need to analyse yourself and think of how you could have dealt with it differently and resolved it so you don't carry any negative baggage into the next day.

The key to a happier life is this: *Do not leave any loose ends (unresolved conflicts) when you retire for the day, as they will entangle and make situations worse.*

Let there be no conflict within yourself. Writing in this diary will bring an immediate shift of your focus to the positive aspect, which will help you break the emotional negative loops that you unconsciously get into.

After a stressful day, you should think and write, 'Even though the day was stressful, I did the best I could, and now I deserve to rest. I let go of this long day so I can sleep peacefully.'

So instead of spending all night tossing and turning in pain and agony, *won't it actually be right to let the day go?*

Trust me, it is the only way to end a long day.

Here, this diary will help you develop some positive habits and help you lead a better life. Just spending a few minutes writing in this diary will start changing you and then will eventually transform your life.

Before we go ahead, you need to analyse *your thinking habit.*

Change Your Thinking Habit

Ninety-nine percent of failures come from
people who have the habit of making excuses.
George Washington Carver

WHAT IS YOUR THINKING HABIT? It only matters
when you are undergoing some trials and tribulations in your life,
because during happy times, people are, by default, in a positive state
of mind.

It is true that situations control and influence our thought
processes. There are problems, challenges, and crises coming from
nowhere. Then we all wish for a superpower which can help us
control or tackle difficult situations. We wonder, *How can I control
such situations? How should I handle them? How can I tackle them?*

Let me tell you: YOU CAN'T HANDLE THEM.

Not now and NEVER. You have always been looking for ways to
tackle these situations. Sadly, you have been searching for something
which doesn't exist.

Then why are some people a success and others rarely taste it?

Do successful people have better capacities, talents, and abilities?

In the *Mahabharata* war, were the Pandavas more powerful than
the Kauravas, whom they defeated?

No, a big NO!

Every Kaurava was equally as powerful and talented as the Pandavas, if not more.

Then what made the difference?

It is not only the talent or the abilities but also the swiftness with which you transform yourself to face any given situation that can determine your success. The only thing a person has to do is transform his own self—that is, the way he analyses the situations and develops innovative thinking—to become a success.

Sometimes it is absolutely impossible to handle a crisis. How can you handle something which you don't have control over?

What if the economy is declining, there are no job opportunities, you are not able to find a suitable match for yourself, your relationships have gone for a toss, the entrance exam is really difficult to crack, the rates of shares are going down, and earthquakes or floods have hit your city?

Can you control these situations? No! So what do you do? How do you face these challenges? How do you rise above these crises?

You have to TRANSFORM YOURSELF to overcome them.

I am sure you have played video games or a mobile game where you are racing a car and want to reach the finishing line but there are several obstacles in between. There are potholes and other cars on the road; some of them are moving right and left. All of a sudden, you run out of fuel. So how do you tackle these problems?

You just try to move away from them, don't you? You change your course and take a left or right, increase or decrease the speed, and try to avoid an accident, and finally, you reach the destination. The fastest racer is the WINNER.

- ➢ the one who takes the least time to reach the goal
- ➢ the one who changes his strategy with the coming challenges more quickly than the others
- ➢ the one who doesn't grumble or complain about the challenges
- ➢ the one who is alert, focused, and ready to TRANSFORM

> ➤ the one who increases or decreases the speed of the car as and when required
> ➤ the one who is not scared of the unexpected challenges

This is the one who can be a success. It is not that the other players are less talented or have not played enough or are unlucky. They too could have been the WINNER.

Then what stopped them?

> ➤ They take more time to think and do not respond quickly.
> ➤ While playing the game, whenever they come across a challenge, like a sudden pothole or a car moving suddenly to the left or right, they grumble, complain, and feel sad and upset. They just want a smooth path to the destination, which is far from reality.
> ➤ They are not alert about the changes; they lack focus and don't change their route accordingly.
> ➤ They don't know when to increase the speed and when to decrease, they are unable to make the most out of the opportunities.
> ➤ They are scared to face the situations, and they slow down and run out of fuel and can never reach the finishing line.

So how do *you* think? Like a winner or a loser?

Which personality traits do you possess?

What is stopping you from being a success?

Why does your friend, your competitor, or your neighbour have a better lifestyle than you?

What is it that they did and you didn't?

You should begin this transformation process by knowing yourself: WHO ARE YOU?

Who Are You?

Nobody is superior, nobody is inferior,
but nobody is equal either.
People are simply unique, incomparable.
You are you, I am I.

Osho

Yes! You are truly different, amazing, and unique. So, there is no question of comparison. But aren't we always judgemental about others? We often claim to know them very well. We judge others by their behaviour. We don't hesitate to comment on their attitude, their behaviour, and even their way of life. We have loads of suggestions for them. But growth lies not in knowing others; it is in knowing oneself.

The power lies within us, but to unlock it, we need to know ourselves first.

So, my friend, let us discover ourselves. Let me help you in doing this.

Have you ever played chess? I am sure you have. Even if you haven't, you probably know at least the basics.

Chess is played by two players, and both begin equally, with the same resources. Each player has eight pawns (soldiers), two knights (horses), two bishops (camels), two rooks (elephants), one queen, and one king.

Each player has to make a choice: whom to risk and whom to protect. In order to protect the king and the queen, pawns, knights, rooks, and bishops are sacrificed, if needed. The mission is to save their own king and challenge the king of the other player.

Each of these chess pieces is very unique, just like we are.

The knight. This chess piece moves in a very special and different manner: it has the power to move two and a half steps and jump over any other piece on the board.

The bishop and the rook. The bishop moves diagonally, whereas the rook moves straight, either horizontally or vertically. Both can't change their movement, though they can both go both forward and backward.

The pawn. This piece can only move one step forward at a time and attack only one step diagonally. The pawn has no choice but to go forward; it cannot go back. But if the pawn reaches the last square, then it can be replaced with any other chess piece, like a knight, a bishop, a rook, or even a queen. It can transform itself into any of them and become a *game changer.*

The queen. This is the most powerful one, as it can move any number of steps, horizontally, vertically, or diagonally, but it can't move like a knight.

The king. It usually moves only when challenged by the opponent. It can move only one step in any direction to save itself.

Let's now understand the game of our life with the help of chess.

The queen. I would call the queen of chess any person who is multitalented, resourceful, and very powerful, as the queen can move in any direction it pleases. It can move as many squares as it wants and can even go ahead and come back to its safe territory. When the queen is on the hunt, the opposite player has to be very alert and cautious.

But even the queen is not unconquerable. It has one limitation. It cannot move like a knight can. So if the player is aware of this weakness and accepts it and then moves the queen with care, only then can the queen be the game changer. Or else, even though it is the most powerful, it could be out of the game quickly.

So, even if you are multitalented and powerful like the queen, you should be aware of your limitation and acknowledge the fact that your overconfidence can kill you. Often, it is seen that the one who is consistently winning at various levels is unable to crack the finals, unless he TRANSFORMS his attitude from being overconfident to being a learner.

The knight. I would call the knight of chess any person who is gifted with an innate ability, a blessed one who has some exceptional talent which no one else has, as the knight is the only one that can move in a unique way: two and a half steps. And to be different is a powerful quality.

Though special, the knight also has a limitation: it cannot move for more than two and a half steps at a time to save himself or attack another.

So if you are the knight, you have a talent for doing something very differently. We see some shows on TV where such people showcase their talent, but they can do nothing else other than that. They get trapped in their own image, profession, or culture, unless they TRANSFORM.

The bishop and the rook. I would call any person who has the power to leave an impact on the world, a bishop or a rook. They have a specific direction to move. The bishop moves diagonally, whereas the rook moves either horizontally or vertically. They both can attack from any distance and go back to their safe territory. Such people avoid taking risks. They simply look for an opportunity to hit and then move back, waiting for another one. But such people are often sacrificed to save the queen or the king. These are the loyal ones, the ones that never break any rule.

Now imagine if the bishop could TRANSFORM into the rook or vice versa. Then how different would the game and life be?

Don't get trapped in the belief that you can only work in a specific way. TRANSFORM and enjoy the variety of life. You can adopt a new way while retaining your earlier powers.

Diversify—to exist, to live, to thrive.

The pawn. These are the people who have limited resources and talent—*the born ordinary.* They have no great achievement in their childhood or in their teens. They were born into an ordinary family background. They don't possess any special talent and are mostly sacrificed to protect the big ones, the rich ones, the powerful ones. The pawn can only move one step ahead. In a crisis, it can't even go back. It can only move ahead in a straight direction. But it can have small successes on its way by attacking in one diagonal move.

However, if this pawn reaches the last square, surviving all the odds, then it can TRANSFORM into anything that it desires to win the game of life. It can become a knight, a bishop, a rook, or even the queen.

Now think, if you were born as a pawn with limited resources—no great education, no influential family background, not economically strong. If you just have patience and keep on doing your job with dedication, determination, and unparalleled focus and you grab the opportunities as they come, then no one can stop you from TRANSFORMING yourself into a great achiever.

A pawn is like a grain of sand, trivial and unimportant, but if it reaches inside the shell of an oyster, it will TRANSFORM into a pearl one day—a lustrous white invaluable pearl! (Like APJ Abdul Kalam, Dhirubhai Ambani, Mahatma Gandhi, or Narendra Modi.)

The king. This is the most important one, the blessed, the crowned, and the game of chess is all about protecting the king. The king has an entire team which is willing to protect it, even if they have to sacrifice themselves in the process. The king is a silent spectator who watches the game in a passive way. It doesn't matter to the king whether it has lost a knight or a bishop or even the queen; the king mostly acts when it is challenged by the opposite player. Though it is the king, it doesn't have the ability to save its own army. It can only move one step on either side. *How restricted!*

Now think of a person who is like a king, who has a number of people to protect him, and who is completely dependent on them for his survival. Sadly, he does not acquire any skill or talent in the entire journey, and he stays inactive in all situations, good or bad. Finally, he *wins* or *loses* without having learnt anything, or achieving much.

Now who doesn't wish to live like a king and enjoy all the privileges? But what's the use of being a king if he remains completely dependent on others, and is unable to discover his own power? Now think of how different the game of chess would be if the so-called king was so powerful that he could protect not only himself but also his army!

Even he needs to be TRANSFORMED to acquire all the necessary skills to live a worthy life. So if you are blessed to have been born into a family of riches, fame, or genius, if a bunch of people are ready to work for you and protect you; but if you don't acquire the necessary skills or TRANSFORM or act and make the necessary decisions at the right time, you lose all your glory.

Many such *kings* could not continue their family's legacy, as they couldn't discover their own potential and abilities, and succumbed under the burden of their parents' success.

The two players who play this game of chess. The one who has the white pieces begins first. The player with white pieces has the right to make the first move, but it doesn't mean that the player with the black pieces has less chances of winning.

So now think: whether you start working on your ideas, ambitions, desires or wishes at an early stage or a little later, it would not make much of a difference. You too can make it BIG!

The day you decide to TRANSFORM your thoughts, you have already set the wheels in motion. Your chances of succeeding are no less, like Boman Irani, a well-known actor who started his film career when he was forty-three.

So how do you define your identity?

_____

_____

_____

For example: 'I am a loving, caring, and happy person.'

Now add to your identity statement those qualities which can help you transform into a better human being. You just have to focus on being one. Just keep on repeating it every day until it becomes the truth of your life.

_____

_____

_____

For example: 'I am a loving, caring, and happy person. I can take the decisions of my life. I am able to speak my mind. I am a confident person. I am the master of my life. I am a responsible person. I am passionate about my work.'

Now that you have defined your biggest challenge, your identity statement, you can take the next step. Analyse *who influences your decisions—the head or the heart?*

Who Rules—The Head Or The Heart?

It doesn't matter what people think of you
as long as you know that
your heart and head are in the right place.

Steve Kluger

Peple have always argued about who should rule our life—THE HEAD OR THE HEART? When you have to make decisions, which one are you -- more logical or more emotional? Thinking should always be scientific and based on reason, but the final decision should be made by your heart. What you feel is much more important when you are at the crossroads, making choices in your life. Your emotions, feelings, and intuition always show you the right path. *But are you listening?*

Remember, the head thinks, but the heart knows. So try to strike the right balance between the two.

Thinking Pattern

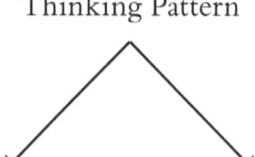

Scientific and logical   Emotions/ Feelings
(Go with your brain)   (Go with your heart)

A student trying to crack a competitive exam cannot do it with only positive feelings; on the contrary, he has to prepare himself systematically and logically for the exam. However, during the exam, he may rely on his intuition when he is confused in choosing the correct answer.

While playing games or sports also, one has to use the scientific method or logic for every move one makes, so that one can attempt to win the game without breaking the rules. However, the right attitude, positive approach, and body language of a player can have an impact on the psychology of his opponent. It is often observed that the people who put their heart into their work can do miracles. So when you attach emotions to your work, you tend to create magic in your actions and words, and thus, you have more chances to win the game.

In the Mahabharata, when Yudhishthira and his brothers were invited to play Chausar by Duryodhana, Mama Shakuni rolled the dice for Duryodhana, and Yudhishthira willingly allowed that with all his love, though the rule of the game is that the one who plays has to roll the dice.

And we know the later part of the story where Yudhishthira lost everything, including his wife, his brothers, and himself too.

So only emotions and feelings are not always helpful. If he had refused to allow Shakuni Mama to roll the dice instead of Duryodhana, then the result would have been different.

Now the question is, *how to find the right balance between the two?*

Let all the pros and cons, advantages and disadvantages, profit and loss be considered in your scientific and logical mind.

Let all the strategies be planned accordingly.

Let all research be made, information gathered, laws studied, and a plan made consciously and meticulously.

But then invoke your heart and listen to your inner voice. It will guide you through all the obstacles and make you a success.

Let all this be done with a much-needed ingredient: *acceptance.*

Acceptance

The first step of TRANSFORMATION is ACCEPTANCE.

Acceptance means:
> For now, this is what this situation,
> this moment, requires me to do
> and so, I do it willingly.
>
> Eckhart Tolle

It's true that the first step is the most difficult one to take. Have you seen a young baby trying to take his first step? His parents make him stand, coax him, persuade him, or lure him with a toy or a chocolate to make him take his first step and try to walk. But the child is scared and nervous, not ready for it. He then cries, yells, stays inactive, or simply sits down or starts crawling. Yes! We too do the same.

Cry: We grumble, complain, or criticise how the change can be difficult, tiring, exhausting, and nerve-racking.

Yell: We keep on telling our friends and family how and why change is not needed; we want to convince others that we are right and that the rest are all wrong.

Stay inactive: We become passive. We are so confused and nervous that we just are not able to decide what to do and whether to change the course of life or not. We simply stand at that juncture of life too long.

Sit down: We just withdraw from the situation and sit back, take a step back, and try to clarify that we are not ready for any change.

Crawl: We don't want to change or undergo transformation, so we just do what we can do easily, without putting in any extra effort—crawl, stay safe, feel secure, and not try a new way of life.

The child doesn't know that taking that one step can change his entire life. So he hesitates. But why are you hesitating? Remember, the only way to bring about a desired change in your life is to take the first step, which is to ACCEPT.

ACCEPT WHAT?

- ➢ ACCEPT your current situation.
- ➢ ACCEPT that no one else is responsible for your current life.
- ➢ ACCEPT that you need to TRANSFORM.

ACCEPT that YOU and only YOU can TRANSFORM YOUR life.

ACCEPT that if you change your thought process and working style, then you can bring a greater and better change in your life.

ACCEPT that writing in this diary every day for a few minutes can put you into a TRANSFORMATION MODE.

ACCEPT your family, your friends, and your work atmosphere, and just focus on transforming yourself.

You can start with affirmations like:

a) I accept myself, and I am now ready to transform into a higher being.
b) I accept my current income and am ready for a higher income flowing towards me.
c) I accept my physical health and am ready to improve it day by day in every way.

Accept your current life and aim to change it.

I accept my _____

_____

*Your name:*_____

*Date:*_____

The key is to accept the current situation, become aware of and choose your destination, and change your direction to reach there and take the next step, which is to ACT.

Act

ACT NOW AND FOREVER

Every pro was once an amateur
Every expert was once a beginner
So, dream big and start now.

Unknown

*C*ongratulations! You have reached the next level and are a step closer to success. You have successfully *accepted* your present, and now it is time to TRANSFORM and take the next step, which is to ACT. Don't miss this moment, this excitement, this day. Gear up and prepare to ACT.

You might be wondering:

➤ How do I gear up?
➤ How do I prepare to ACT?
➤ What should I do?

Before you discover the answers to those, let's see if you can answer this question: *What is the one place where you can see all types of cars, except on roads?* ('All types' means from the most expensive and luxurious to the cheapest one in the market, even an old model or a second-hand car.)

Yes! You guessed it right! A petrol pump or a gas station.

Yes! Any car you own is of no use if it doesn't have fuel in it, isn't that right? All the comforts, luxuries, brands, interiors, and the best technologies and dynamics are an absolute ZERO if your car runs short of FUEL. So it's the FUEL that is the soul, the energy of the car.

Similarly, to be a success, after accepting your present, the FUEL needed for gearing up and moving ahead is the ACTION you take, the EFFORT you make towards TRANSFORMATION.

Let me share with you how I learnt to take action and made one of my wishes come true.

I had started working in an institute as a visiting lecturer. Since I didn't have any vehicle of my own, I had to spend an insane amount of time travelling by public transport. Then one day, I thought of buying my own two-wheeler, but I didn't have that much money.

Every day I would look down from the window and *visualise* my bike standing there. I used to feel highly excited about it. After a few days, I decided to ACT on my wish. I asked my mother-in-law to give me a loan of Rs.50,000, and she agreed. In a week's time, I had my wish fulfilled. Later, I repaid my loan in instalments.

What if I had not ACTED? What if I had not asked for a loan?

Asking and acting is the next step to fulfilling your goals. *Ask* 'How can I get it done?' And then ACT on the path you have chosen. So FUEL your desires with ACTION.

You have already taken one ACTION by choosing to read this book, which will help you in your journey to success.

Now try to answer my next question: *What can stop you from driving your car even if it has enough fuel and is in very good working condition?* Hmm! It is difficult to guess.

The answer is YOU. If you have all the resources, talent, and knowledge but lack the *desire, the burning desire* to achieve your goal, nothing can help you then.

THE DESIRE TO TRANSFORM IS ALL YOU NEED TO ACT.

Writing in this diary every day will ensure that you fuel your *desire* every day. You remind yourself of what you want and motivate yourself. You can write affirmations like:

1. I am buying a car for myself by December.
2. I want a promotion in my job and am working sincerely for it.
3. I am losing weight through a healthy diet, positive thinking, and exercise.

(Note that you should write in the continuous tense related to present time.)

When you ACT, you ARISE.

Arise

Arise! Awake! And stop not till the goal is reached.
Swami Vivekananda

Better days are coming. You have been through a lot. Now it's time for you to shine.

Each one of us wants to ARISE, wants to place one's own self in a better position and situation. Still everyone doesn't seem to succeed, just because they are not doing *what is required*.

Let us understand this. We have seen many airplanes flying high, birds swiftly soaring, rockets shooting up, and many more such dynamics.

What is it that helps them do so? All of them aim to *arise* and reach a higher level.

In order to *arise*, you need to be *aligned*. Only if all the aspects are aligned can you *arise*. Yes! Let me repeat that: *only if all the aspects are aligned can one arise.*

What are these aspects?

All those conditions, systems, and mechanisms required for flying. In the case of an airplane, it means all the technology and machinery must be in working condition. It includes weather, movement of wind, dynamics, and timing, when all these are aligned (meaning they work together), then the airplane flies or *arises*.

But how can we *arise*? Only if every aspect needed for it is aligned—that is, if you are at the same frequency as of your dreams.

Let us understand this concept of FREQUENCY. Every thought, wish, desire, or dream has its own frequency, just like a radio station. Whenever we wish to listen to a particular radio channel, don't we TUNE in to that channel's FREQUENCY? For example, if I want to listen to 94.5 FM, I have to TUNE my radio to it; only then can the radio catch the signals, and I can hear the programme.

In the same way, only if we TUNE in to the frequency of our DESIRE or DREAM can the results be seen or manifested. If you wish to gain some profit from the share market, now that's your WISH, and to make this wish come true, you need to TUNE yourself to get it.

1. You need to have a Demat account.
2. You need to contact a share broker.
3. You need to understand the workings of the share market.
4. You need to research about the company you want to invest in.
5. You need to invest money in some scripts.
6. You need to keenly observe the price each day.
7. You need to stay in contact with your broker.
8. The timing of investment is important, as one should not buy when the prices are too high.
9. You need to have faith, have courage, have patience… and it will work.

Though there may be many unforeseen factors that also work for your success, you have to follow the BASICS. You have to TUNE in to the BASICS.

There are also chances that you have tuned in to the right frequency to listen to the radio, but maybe the signals are not reaching you or there is some error from the radio station or adverse weather conditions have obstructed the transmission; however, all these are not in your control, so you can't help but bear with them.

So to be a success, one needs to do two things:

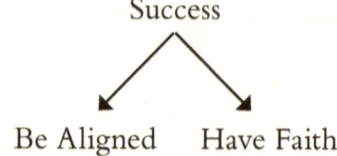

Success

Be Aligned   Have Faith

In other words, to make money in the share market, you have to follow the BASICS and have FAITH that it will work.

FAITH in the Universe.
FAITH in the Supreme Energy.
FAITH in the Divine.
FAITH in God.
FAITH in Your Efforts.
FAITH in Yourself.
FAITH that all is WELL.

This FAITH will protect you from all unforeseen circumstances. Having FAITH will take you to another level.

In *Shrimad Bhagwad Gita*, it is said:

Karmanye vadhikaraste, Ma phaleshou kada chana,
Ma karma phala heturbhur, Matey sangostva akarmani.

This simply means 'Do your *karma* or *deeds*'; it means follow the BASICS and don't worry about the *fruits* or the *result*. That is, once you have done the required action, have FAITH in the universe, in the divine, that it will work.

So before you start your day, invoke the divine. You can write affirmations like:

1. The divine energy is with me.
2. God is guiding me all the time.
3. I am guided by the divine and thus am on the path of success.

(You may write these affirmations in your mother tongue, and you may name God or the Guru or any such divine energy you have faith in.)

While we invoke the divine and wish to achieve more, we should also *be grateful* for what we have.

Be Grateful

I may not be where I want to be,
But thank God I am not where I used to be.

Joyce Meyer

A *thank you* is what is needed to conclude.

To conclude your prayers, your wishes, your dreams, and your life.

Your journey in this world has been so unique, so different to date that you just need to be *thankful*. You are the only one of your own self. You are not just limited edition; you are actually unique!

Doesn't this fact make your life so special?

There are many things in our life that we have inherited, many things that we never asked for. We may think, 'Why am I in such situations, with such people or such a family background, culture, or country?'

We may not have answers to these questions, but we have the power to change such situations. This is where we get the motive of our life. This is when we start weaving our dreams, our desires, and the goals of our life.

These challenges make us *grow*, make us *powerful*, and give us the will to *rise*, to *stretch our hands*, to *touch the skies*.

So don't you think these problems, obstacles, and situations are blessings in disguise? Yes, they are, but we realise it only later!

Life is like a treasure hunt.

Haven't you seen movies or read books or even played games based on treasure hunts?

How exciting they are!

All of us are pursuing a goal, *a treasure*!

It is a *treasure* which is unseen, unknown, but we have imagined its grandeur.

There are several clues, puzzles, mazes, and obstacles that you need to overcome in order to reach the *treasure*. Sometimes you feel you have reached the *treasure*, but it is just an illusion. Many times, you reach your desired destination, but it's at an unexpected time.

So that's how life is. We have our dreams, desires, wishes, and a lot more, but we have to face several troubles, challenges, and situations which need sheer courage. Facing them and overcoming them *transforms* you into a better person. Whether you achieve your set goal or not, the experience is overwhelming. This experience is certainly a stepping stone to the next phase of your life.

Whether the experience is good or bad, it is at least an excellent teacher, so don't you feel you should be grateful for it?

Even if you fail, you can still

- *be grateful* for the strength you had for the hard work
- *be grateful* you had the courage to try your idea, because many have died without even trying for what they believed
- *be grateful* for the friends you made along this journey, many new acquaintances who might become great pals in the future
- *be grateful* for the lessons you learnt from this experience, as they are so deeply engraved in your heart that you can never forget them.

And if you have been *successful*, then *every moment, every time, every day* you *must be grateful* for it. It is not just you who made it happen; many factors played a crucial role in it.

The more you are grateful for, the more you will get to be grateful for.

Try this amazing technique: every time you find something good happening, be *grateful*.

Thank the almighty God. Thank those people who have helped you in that achievement. Thank the situations that helped you.

Now just be a little alert in your life, and soon you will find more such incidents for which you will be *grateful* again!

Let me share with you an amazing incident of my life when I truly experienced *the power of gratitude*.

My daughter was going to sit for her SSC exam. Obviously, she was a little stressed, though she was quite prepared. It was her algebra exam. I wanted to cheer her up, so I just randomly asked her to praise her teachers who had taught her algebra. I asked her to say 'Vipin Sir *ki jai*', 'Sailee Miss *ki jai*', and '*Jo Algebra padhaye, uski jai*'.

The entire time I was driving her to her exam centre, we kept on repeating the above praises. It sounded ridiculously funny, but she found it relaxing; she was smiling. Then she took her exam.

Later it became a ritual; in all the remaining exams, we did that on the way to her exam centre. Her exams went well. She scored a whopping 92%. I had forgotten all about the praises that we sang during exams. Then one day, some two years later, when we were just talking casually, she said that she still continues that ritual, and in her college exams too, she did the same, remembering her teachers and thanking them and singing their praises. Then I realised how just thanking sincerely can be so powerful that she always got more opportunities to be thankful!

Sincere gratitude from the bottom of your heart will empower you to become what you want to be.

So every day, count your blessings when you wake up and before you go to sleep.

You can express your gratitude for even the simplest and humblest things which we often overlook, like:

- Thank you, God, for this beautiful sunny morning.
- Thank you, God, for the food I ate today.
- Thank you, God, for I made a new friend today.

- Thank you, Mom, for loving me so much.
- Thank you, my dear husband, for supporting me in my work.

Feeling gratitude and not expressing it is like wrapping a present and not giving it. (William Arthur Ward)

Finally, after *gratitude*, we should believe in *blessings* too.

Blessings

When you focus on being a blessing,
God makes sure that you are always
blessed in abundance.

Joel Osteen

A blessing is an elixir, like *Amrit* for our life. In India, we always look for *blessings*. We staunchly believe that the *blessings* of our parents, teachers, gurus, and elders can sometimes be the saviour of our life. *Blessings* can be given and received.

It is true that good deeds attract *blessings*, but still, we cannot be sure about receiving them.

The amazing thing about *blessings* is that *we can always bless others.* At least we can bring a smile to someone's face and make him feel good and positive with our *blessings*. A wholehearted blessing to someone who is special to us or someone for whom we are concerned can definitely inspire him, make him hopeful, or fill him with immense joy.

Blessings really are magical!

We have heard of several mythological stories where these *blessings* have changed the course of someone's life. But many of you might not believe in these stories. Then, my friend, let me tell you that even today, when we go to temples, gurdwaras, churches, mosques, and any such spiritually vibrant place, we do so mainly in search of *blessings*, don't we?

But why are we always seeking *blessings*? Because we know that the Supreme Power, the Almighty, the Divine, can grant us that which we may not have control over.

When someone is critically ill, don't we pray for his speedy recovery, as at that time we are helpless and can't do anything else? When someone has lost a near and dear one, what do we do? Just pray! Because we are helpless.

Praying for oneself or for others is what we naturally do when we want God to intervene or guide us in such situations.

But we hardly know whether our prayers will be answered or not.

Here, I want to tell you, my friend, that when you wish to help yourself or others, along with praying, *do bless them*.

Any act you do, small or big, do it with *blessings*.

If you are giving money to a beggar, say, *'God bless you!'*

If your friend is in trouble, hug him and say, *'God bless you!'*

If your child is ill, caress him and say, *'God bless you!'*

Try to *bless* every person you see, who is in need of it. You will be creating a very positive and healing aura around him. This positivity will definitely encompass and benefit you too.

You can *bless* yourself too. Look into the mirror and say, *'God bless you! God is with you!'*

Begin your day with a smile. Write in this diary *blessings* for yourself and for others too. *Bless* with deep and pure emotions. For example:

- God bless you, my child, with success and happiness.
- God bless you, my friend, with extraordinary health and wealth.

With all the blessings and best wishes, you are now about to experience eternal *magic* in your life. This diary will guide you. So get out of your comfort zone, act and arise, and create *magic*.

Remember,

> Those who don't believe in magic will never find it.
> (Roald Dahl)

Now design your world with a *commitment,* which you will always fulfil. An appointment with this diary, which you will always keep.

My Commitment is my Investment

I, _____ Seema Singh _____, commit to writing in this diary for at least five days in a row, starting from _1 August 2020._

Writing in this diary is really important to me because:

I want to have more abundance in my life.
I want clarity in my life.
I want my dreams to become my reality.

If I write in my diary for the first twenty-one days without any break, then I will reward myself with: an adventurous trip with my friend.

(It is important to understand the fact that to develop any new habit, you should continue that act for at least twenty-one days. This cycle of twenty-one days will start to instil in you the new habit of writing in this diary. The diary has three such cycles, to ensure that you start refining your life and continue this process throughout your life.)

I will do the following things to ensure that I write in this diary every day:

a) I will keep this diary next to my bed.
b) I will set my alarm only after I write in this diary.
c) I will keep all my gadgets aside for some time so I can focus on writing in this diary.
d) I will share this commitment with my sister.

My Commitment is my Investment

(Fill in these blanks with your beliefs and emotions.)

I, _____, commit
to writing in this diary for at least five days in a row, starting
from _____.

Writing in this diary is really important to me because:

_____

_____

_____

If I write in my diary for twenty-one days without a break, then
I will reward myself with:

_____

I will do the following things to ensure that I write in this diary
every day:

a) _____

b) _____

c) _____

d) _____

Design Your Day

Build your own dreams,
Or someone else will hire you to build theirs.

Farrah Gray

Yes, my friend! With all the good wishes, gratitude, intent, and blessings, you can design your day—in fact, every day.

Begin your day with gratitude.
For example:

a) I am grateful for this beautiful day.
b) I am grateful for my wonderful health.
c) I am grateful that I have healthy relations with my family.

By being *grateful*, you are getting the ball rolling, and the more you are *grateful*, the more reasons you will get to be grateful for.

The next thought must be, 'What would make my day special?' Think of all those things that you can possibly do and feel good about.

For example:

a) I will call up my childhood friend today.
b) I will gift a new dress to my wife.
c) I will spend at least fifteen minutes for myself.

Finally, start your day with a *daily affirmation*. You can write any specific wish which you want to come true.

For example:

a) <u>I am feeling happy and passionate about my job.</u>
b) <u>I am earning five lakh rupees every month.</u>
c) <u>I am blessed with love and friendship.</u>

(You may refer to page no. 143 onwards for the list of affirmations.)

> It's the repetition of affirmations that leads to belief.
> And once that belief becomes a deep conviction, things begin to happen. (Muhammad Ali)

As much as it is important to begin your day on a positive note, you must also end the day in a similar way. Before you go to bed, take just a few minutes to write in this diary *what you are grateful for*—anything wonderful that happened that day and that you wish to acknowledge.

Amazing things that happened today:

For example:

a) <u>I am grateful, for I completed my project today.</u>
b) <u>I am grateful, for my teacher praised my efforts.</u>
c) <u>I am grateful to my friend, who helped me.</u>

Now think of any situation which you could have handled in a different way or in an innovative way that day. For example, you had an argument with your friend, and it was bad. You may write:

<u>I wish I had been a little softer in my tone when I was making my point.</u>

Such self-analysis and realisation will surely help you tackle similar situations better, in the future.

Finally, *end your day with a blessing.*

Though you may *bless* people the whole day whenever you feel like doing it, don't retire for the day without *blessing*.

For example: <u>I bless you, my child, with more strength and good health. Get well soon, baby!</u>

<u>God bless my colleagues, who helped me perform better today!</u>

So, dear friend, just don't wait. Take a pen and start *designing your day, your week, your month, your years to come, and your life.*

Define it and refine it.

In whatever stage of life you are, whether a teenager or a senior citizen, you can still add a lot of peace, happiness, and value to your life.

So, my friend, *pick up your pen and pen down your dreams, your feelings, and your passions.* This diary is your friend and your guide, which will help you not only design your world but also record all your beautiful emotions, wishes, and dreams. This is memorabilia which you will treasure forever.

The Memorabilia

May you define and refine your life before you resign!

Day 1

Date: ___/___/20___

The ultimate measure of a man is not where he stands
in moments of comfort and convenience, but where
he stands at times of challenge and controversy.
Martin Luther King Jr

I am grateful for . . .

a) _____

b) _____

What would make my day special?

a) _____

b) _____

Daily affirmation: I am . . .

_____

_____

Amazing things that happened today:

a) _____

b) _____

I could have made this day even better if I had . . .

_____

_____

End your day with a blessing:

_____

_____

Day 2

Date: ___/___/20___

In prayers, it is not how well
you arrange your words,
but how well you arrange your heart that counts.
Pramukh Swami Maharaj

I am grateful for . . .

a) _____

b) _____

What would make my day special?

a) _____

b) _____

Daily affirmation: I am . . .

_____

_____

Amazing things that happened today:

a) _____

b) _____

I could have made this day even better if I had . . .

_____

_____

End your day with a blessing:

_____

_____

Day 3

Date: ___/___/20___

Keep your face always towards the sunshine
and your shadow will fall behind you.
Walt Whitman

I am grateful for . . .

a) _____

b) _____

What would make my day special?

a) _____

b) _____

Daily affirmation: I am . . .

_____

_____

Amazing things that happened today:

a) _____

b) _____

I could have made this day even better if I had . . .

_____

_____

End your day with a blessing:

_____

_____

Day 4

Date: ____/____/20____

Don't go through life, grow through life.

Gopal Prabhu

I am grateful for . . .

a) _____

b) _____

What would make my day special?

a) _____

b) _____

Daily affirmation: I am . . .

_____

_____

Amazing things that happened today:

a) _____

b) _____

I could have made this day even better if I had . . .

_____

_____

End your day with a blessing:

_____

_____

Day 5

Date: ____/____/20____

You cannot handle LARGE opportunities,
if small problems bother you.

Mahatria Ra

I am grateful for . . .

a) _____

b) _____

What would make my day special?

a) _____

b) _____

Daily affirmation: I am . . .

_____

_____

Amazing things that happened today:

a) _____

b) _____

I could have made this day even better if I had . . .

_____

_____

End your day with a blessing:

_____

_____

Day 6

Date: ___/___/20___

If you don't fight for what you want,
don't cry for what you lost.
Shrimad Bhagvad Gita

I am grateful for . . .

a) _____

b) _____

What would make my day special?

a) _____

b) _____

Daily affirmation: I am . . .

_____

_____

Amazing things that happened today:

a) _____

b) _____

I could have made this day even better if I had . . .

_____

_____

End your day with a blessing:

_____

_____

Weekly Challenge

(Go to the list of weekly challenges on page no. 141, pick any one of the challenges, and go for it!)

Day 7

Date: ___/___/20___

Change happens when the pain of staying the same
is greater than the pain of change.

Tony Robbins

I am grateful for . . .

a) _____

b) _____

What would make my day special?

a) _____

b) _____

Daily affirmation: I am . . .

_____

_____

Amazing things that happened today:

a) _____

b) _____

I could have made this day even better if I had . . .

_____

_____

End your day with a blessing:

_____

_____

Day 8

Date: ___/___/20___

Postpone joy, it will diminish;
postpone a problem, it will grow.
                              Paulo Coelho

I am grateful for . . .

a) _____

b) _____

What would make my day special?

a) _____

b) _____

Daily affirmation: I am . . .

_____

_____

Amazing things that happened today:

a) _____

b) _____

I could have made this day even better if I had . . .

_____

_____

End your day with a blessing:

_____

_____

Day 9

Date: ___/___/20___

Faith is to believe what you do not yet see;
the reward for this faith is to see what you believe.
Saint Augustine

I am grateful for . . .

a) _____

b) _____

What would make my day special?

a) _____

b) _____

Daily affirmation: I am . . .

_____

_____

Amazing things that happened today:

a) _____

b) _____

I could have made this day even better if I had . . .

_____

_____

End your day with a blessing:

_____

_____

Day 10

Date: ___/___/20___

What a wonderful life I've had!
I only wish I'd realised it sooner.
Sidonie-Gabrielle Colette

I am grateful for . . .

a) _____

b) _____

What would make my day special?

a) _____

b) _____

Daily affirmation: I am . . .

_____

_____

Amazing things that happened today:

a) _____

b) _____

I could have made this day even better if I had . . .

_____

_____

End your day with a blessing:

_____

_____

Day 11

Date: ___/___/20___

Spread love everywhere you go. Let no one
ever come to you without leaving happier.

Saint Teresa

I am grateful for . . .

a) _____

b) _____

What would make my day special?

a) _____

b) _____

Daily affirmation: I am . . .

_____

_____

Amazing things that happened today:

a) _____

b) _____

I could have made this day even better if I had . . .

_____

_____

End your day with a blessing:

_____

_____

Day 12

Date: ___/___/20___

Only the fear of diving could have
stopped you from finding the pearls.
Chaitali Mehta

I am grateful for . . .

a) _____

b) _____

What would make my day special?

a) _____

b) _____

Daily affirmation: I am . . .

_____

_____

Amazing things that happened today:

a) _____

b) _____

I could have made this day even better if I had . . .

_____

_____

End your day with a blessing:

_____

_____

Day 13

Date: ____/____/20____

There are two ways of spreading light;
to be the candle or the mirror that reflects it.

Edith Wharton

I am grateful for . . .

a) _____

b) _____

What would make my day special?

a) _____

b) _____

Daily affirmation: I am . . .

_____

_____

Amazing things that happened today:

a) _____

b) _____

I could have made this day even better if I had . . .

_____

_____

End your day with a blessing:

_____

_____

Weekly Challenge

(Go to the list of weekly challenges on page no. 141,
pick any one of the challenges, and go for it!)

Day 14

Date: ____/____/20____

There is more hunger for love and
appreciation in this world than for bread.

Saint Teresa

I am grateful for . . .

a) _____

b) _____

What would make my day special?

a) _____

b) _____

Daily affirmation: I am . . .

_____

_____

Amazing things that happened today:

a) _____

b) _____

I could have made this day even better if I had . . .

_____

_____

End your day with a blessing:

_____

_____

Day 15

Date: ____/____/20____

A ship is safe in harbour,
but that's not what ships are for.

John A. Shedd

I am grateful for . . .

a) _____

b) _____

What would make my day special?

a) _____

b) _____

Daily affirmation: I am . . .

_____

_____

Amazing things that happened today:

a) _____

b) _____

I could have made this day even better if I had . . .

_____

_____

End your day with a blessing:

_____

_____

Day 16

Date: ___/___/20___

To the world, you may be just one person,
but to one person, you may be the world.
H. Jackson Brown

I am grateful for . . .

a) _____

b) _____

What would make my day special?

a) _____

b) _____

Daily affirmation: I am . . .

_____

_____

Amazing things that happened today:

a) _____

b) _____

I could have made this day even better if I had . . .

_____

_____

End your day with a blessing:

_____

_____

Day 17

Date: ____/____/20____

On my own I will just create, and if it
works, it works, and if it doesn't,
I'll create something else. I don't have any
limitations on what I think I could do or be.

Oprah Winfrey

I am grateful for . . .

a) _____

b) _____

What would make my day special?

a) _____

b) _____

Daily affirmation: I am . . .

_____

_____

Amazing things that happened today:

a) _____

b) _____

I could have made this day even better if I had . . .

_____

_____

End your day with a blessing:

_____

_____

Day 18

Date: ___/___/20___

If you want to go fast, go alone.
If you want to go far, go together.

African proverb

I am grateful for . . .

a) _____

b) _____

What would make my day special?

a) _____

b) _____

Daily affirmation: I am . . .

_____

_____

Amazing things that happened today:

a) _____

b) _____

I could have made this day even better if I had . . .

_____

_____

End your day with a blessing:

_____

_____

Day 19

Date: ___/___/20___

Never complain about the difficulties of life
because the Director (Bappa) always gives
the hardest roles to the Best actors.
Pramukh Swami Maharaj

I am grateful for . . .

a) _____

b) _____

What would make my day special?

a) _____

b) _____

Daily affirmation: I am . . .

_____

_____

Amazing things that happened today:

a) _____

b) _____

I could have made this day even better if I had . . .

_____

_____

End your day with a blessing:

_____

_____

Day 20

Date: ___/___/20___

The sole purpose of education is to
turn mirrors into windows
where you can see others and learn from them.
Chaitali Mehta

I am grateful for . . .

a) _____

b) _____

What would make my day special?

a) _____

b) _____

Daily affirmation: I am . . .

_____

_____

Amazing things that happened today:

a) _____

b) _____

I could have made this day even better if I had . . .

_____

_____

End your day with a blessing:

_____

_____

Weekly Challenge

(Go to the list of weekly challenges on page no. 141,
pick any one of the challenges, and go for it!)

Day 21

Date: ____/____/20____

There is only one success: To be able to
spend your life in your own way.
Christopher Morley

I am grateful for . . .

a) _____

b) _____

What would make my day special?

a) _____

b) _____

Daily affirmation: I am . . .

_____

_____

Amazing things that happened today:

a) _____

b) _____

I could have made this day even better if I had . . .

_____

_____

End your day with a blessing:

_____

_____

Congratulations! You have completed the first cycle successfully.
Now begin with the second cycle.

Day 22

Date: ____/____/20____

My aim is not to do great things but
to do small things in a great way.
Savjibhai Dholakia

I am grateful for . . .

a) _____

b) _____

What would make my day special?

a) _____

b) _____

Daily affirmation: I am . . .

_____

_____

Amazing things that happened today:

a) _____

b) _____

I could have made this day even better if I had . . .

_____

_____

End your day with a blessing:

_____

_____

Day 23

Date: ___/___/20___

None of us really changes over time. We
only become more fully what we are.

Anne Rice

I am grateful for . . .

a) _____

b) _____

What would make my day special?

a) _____

b) _____

Daily affirmation: I am . . .

_____

_____

Amazing things that happened today:

a) _____

b) _____

I could have made this day even better if I had . . .

_____

_____

End your day with a blessing:

_____

_____

Day 24

Date: ___/___/20___

The things that are impossible with
men are possible with God.

The Bible

I am grateful for . . .

a) _____

b) _____

What would make my day special?

a) _____

b) _____

Daily affirmation: I am . . .

_____

_____

Amazing things that happened today:

a) _____

b) _____

I could have made this day even better if I had . . .

_____

_____

End your day with a blessing:

_____

_____

Day 25

Date: ____/____/20____

A thankful heart is not only the greatest virtue,
but the parent of all the other virtues.

Cicero

I am grateful for . . .

a) _____

b) _____

What would make my day special?

a) _____

b) _____

Daily affirmation: I am . . .

_____

_____

Amazing things that happened today:

a) _____

b) _____

I could have made this day even better if I had . . .

_____

_____

End your day with a blessing:

_____

_____

Day 26

Date: ___/___/20___

Mind is never a problem, *Mindset* is!

Narendra Modi

I am grateful for . . .

a) _____

b) _____

What would make my day special?

a) _____

b) _____

Daily affirmation: I am . . .

_____

_____

Amazing things that happened today:

a) _____

b) _____

I could have made this day even better if I had . . .

_____

_____

End your day with a blessing:

_____

_____

Weekly Challenge

(Go to the list of weekly challenges on page no. 141,
pick any one of the challenges, and go for it!)

Day 27

Date: ____/____/20____

Talent hits a target no one else can hit;
genius hits a target no one else can see.

Arthur Schopenhauer

I am grateful for . . .

a) _____

b) _____

What would make my day special?

a) _____

b) _____

Daily affirmation: I am . . .

_____

_____

Amazing things that happened today:

a) _____

b) _____

I could have made this day even better if I had . . .

_____

_____

End your day with a blessing:

_____

_____

Day 28

Date: ___/___/20___

If people throw stones at you,
convert them into milestones.

Sachin Tendulkar

I am grateful for . . .

a) _____

b) _____

What would make my day special?

a) _____

b) _____

Daily affirmation: I am . . .

_____

_____

Amazing things that happened today:

a) _____

b) _____

I could have made this day even better if I had . . .

_____

_____

End your day with a blessing:

_____

_____

Day 29

Date: ____/____/20____

Change is the nature of life, but
challenge is the future of life.
So, challenge the changes, but
never change the challenges.

Amitabh Bachchan

I am grateful for . . .

a) _____

b) _____

What would make my day special?

a) _____

b) _____

Daily affirmation: I am . . .

_____

_____

Amazing things that happened today:

a) _____

b) _____

I could have made this day even better if I had . . .

_____

_____

End your day with a blessing:

_____

_____

Day 30

Date: ____/____/20____

Solve the problem or leave the problem.
But, do not sleep with the problem.

BK Shivani

I am grateful for . . .

a) _____

b) _____

What would make my day special?

a) _____

b) _____

Daily affirmation: I am . . .

_____

_____

Amazing things that happened today:

a) _____

b) _____

I could have made this day even better if I had . . .

_____

_____

End your day with a blessing:

_____

_____

Day 31

Date: ___/___/20___

He, who sows ideas, reaps success.
Chaitali Mehta

I am grateful for . . .

a) _____

b) _____

What would make my day special?

a) _____

b) _____

Daily affirmation: I am . . .

_____

_____

Amazing things that happened today:

a) _____

b) _____

I could have made this day even better if I had . . .

_____

_____

End your day with a blessing:

_____

_____

Day 32

Date: ____/____/20____

If you are NOT AFRAID of losing,
nobody can ever beat you!
Sandeep Maheshwari

I am grateful for . . .

a) _____

b) _____

What would make my day special?

a) _____

b) _____

Daily affirmation: I am . . .

_____

_____

Amazing things that happened today:

a) _____

b) _____

I could have made this day even better if I had . . .

_____

_____

End your day with a blessing:

_____

_____

Day 33

Date: ____/____/20____

If perfection is your goal, you
can achieve it right now;
just stop doing things which are less than perfect.
Chaitali Mehta

I am grateful for . . .

a) _____

b) _____

What would make my day special?

a) _____

b) _____

Daily affirmation: I am . . .

_____

_____

Amazing things that happened today:

a) _____

b) _____

I could have made this day even better if I had . . .

_____

_____

End your day with a blessing:

_____

_____

Weekly Challenge

(Go to the list of weekly challenges on page no. 141,
pick any one of the challenges, and go for it!)

Day 34

Date: ____/____/20____

Without passion, you don't have energy.
Without energy, you have nothing.
Warren Buffett

I am grateful for . . .

a) _____

b) _____

What would make my day special?

a) _____

b) _____

Daily affirmation: I am . . .

_____

_____

Amazing things that happened today:

a) _____

b) _____

I could have made this day even better if I had . . .

_____

_____

End your day with a blessing:

_____

_____

Day 35

Date: ____/____/20____

Opportunity lies in the place
where the complaints are.

Jack Ma

I am grateful for . . .

a) _____

b) _____

What would make my day special?

a) _____

b) _____

Daily affirmation: I am . . .

_____

_____

Amazing things that happened today:

a) _____

b) _____

I could have made this day even better if I had . . .

_____

_____

End your day with a blessing:

_____

_____

Day 36

Date: ____/____/20____

Be successful but not alone;
climb high but not alone,
I have seen many people dying
of success and loneliness.

Chaitali Mehta

I am grateful for . . .

a) _____

b) _____

What would make my day special?

a) _____

b) _____

Daily affirmation: I am . . .

_____

_____

Amazing things that happened today:

a) _____

b) _____

I could have made this day even better if I had . . .

_____

_____

End your day with a blessing:

_____

_____

Day 37

Date: ___/___/20___

Take care of your body. It's the
only place you have to live.

Jim Rohn

I am grateful for . . .

a) _____

b) _____

What would make my day special?

a) _____

b) _____

Daily affirmation: I am . . .

_____

_____

Amazing things that happened today:

a) _____

b) _____

I could have made this day even better if I had . . .

_____

_____

End your day with a blessing:

_____

_____

Day 38

Date: ____/____/20____

If you are helping someone and
expecting something in return,
You are doing business not kindness.

BK Shivani

I am grateful for . . .

a) _____

b) _____

What would make my day special?

a) _____

b) _____

Daily affirmation: I am . . .

_____

_____

Amazing things that happened today:

a) _____

b) _____

I could have made this day even better if I had . . .

_____

_____

End your day with a blessing:

_____

_____

Day 39

Date: ___/___/20___

Being happy doesn't mean that everything is perfect.
It means that you've decided to look
beyond the imperfections.

Amitabh Bachchan

I am grateful for . . .

a) _____

b) _____

What would make my day special?

a) _____

b) _____

Daily affirmation: I am . . .

_____

_____

Amazing things that happened today:

a) _____

b) _____

I could have made this day even better if I had . . .

_____

_____

End your day with a blessing:

_____

_____

Day 40

Date: ___/___/20___

I never stand next to any problem;
I am part of the solution.

Chaitali Mehta

I am grateful for . . .

a) _____

b) _____

What would make my day special?

a) _____

b) _____

Daily affirmation: I am . . .

_____

_____

Amazing things that happened today:

a) _____

b) _____

I could have made this day even better if I had . . .

_____

_____

End your day with a blessing:

_____

_____

Weekly Challenge

(Go to the list of weekly challenges on page no. 141,
pick any one of the challenges, and go for it!)

Day 41

Date: ___/___/20___

Don't be pushed by your problems,
be led by your dreams.
Ralph Waldo Emerson

I am grateful for . . .

a) _____

b) _____

What would make my day special?

a) _____

b) _____

Daily affirmation: I am . . .

_____

_____

Amazing things that happened today:

a) _____

b) _____

I could have made this day even better if I had . . .

_____

_____

End your day with a blessing:

_____

_____

Day 42

Date: ___/___/20___

Don't be dead serious about your
life — it's just a play.

Sadguru

I am grateful for . . .

a) _____

b) _____

What would make my day special?

a) _____

b) _____

Daily affirmation: I am . . .

_____

_____

Amazing things that happened today:

a) _____

b) _____

I could have made this day even better if I had . . .

_____

_____

End your day with a blessing:

_____

_____

Congratulations! You have reached the second milestone
of your transformation. The second cycle of twenty-
one days is over. Now with this third cycle, you will
start experiencing the fun and magic of life.

Day 43

Date: ____/____/20____

There are only two possibilities —
Either you will fall or fly.
Give it a try.

Chaitali Mehta

I am grateful for . . .

a) _____

b) _____

What would make my day special?

a) _____

b) _____

Daily affirmation: I am . . .

_____

_____

Amazing things that happened today:

a) _____

b) _____

I could have made this day even better if I had . . .

_____

_____

End your day with a blessing:

_____

_____

Day 44

Date: ___/___/20___

No one can destroy iron, but its own rust!
Likewise, no one can destroy a
person, but his own mindset!

Ratan Tata

I am grateful for . . .

a) _____

b) _____

What would make my day special?

a) _____

b) _____

Daily affirmation: I am . . .

_____

_____

Amazing things that happened today:

a) _____

b) _____

I could have made this day even better if I had . . .

_____

_____

End your day with a blessing:

_____

_____

Day 45

Date: ____/____/20____

There is no greater violence than to
deny the dreams of our children.

Kailash Satyarthi

I am grateful for . . .

a) _____

b) _____

What would make my day special?

a) _____

b) _____

Daily affirmation: I am . . .

_____

_____

Amazing things that happened today:

a) _____

b) _____

I could have made this day even better if I had . . .

_____

_____

End your day with a blessing:

_____

_____

Day 46

Date: ___/___/20___

Man is made by his belief. As he believes, so he is.
Shrimad Bhagvad Gita

I am grateful for . . .

a) _____

b) _____

What would make my day special?

a) _____

b) _____

Daily affirmation: I am . . .

_____

_____

Amazing things that happened today:

a) _____

b) _____

I could have made this day even better if I had . . .

_____

_____

End your day with a blessing:

_____

_____

Weekly Challenge

(Go to the list of weekly challenges on page no. 141,
pick any one of the challenges, and go for it!)

Day 47

Date: ___/___/20___

If you are grateful, I will give you more.
The Koran

I am grateful for . . .

a) _____

b) _____

What would make my day special?

a) _____

b) _____

Daily affirmation: I am . . .

_____

_____

Amazing things that happened today:

a) _____

b) _____

I could have made this day even better if I had . . .

_____

_____

End your day with a blessing:

_____

_____

Day 48

Date: ___/___/20___

Your worst enemy cannot harm you as
much as your own unguarded thoughts.

Buddha

I am grateful for . . .

a) _____

b) _____

What would make my day special?

a) _____

b) _____

Daily affirmation: I am . . .

_____

_____

Amazing things that happened today:

a) _____

b) _____

I could have made this day even better if I had . . .

_____

_____

End your day with a blessing:

_____

_____

Day 49

Date: ___/___/20___

Always wrong persons teach the right lessons of life.

Buddha

I am grateful for . . .

a) _____

b) _____

What would make my day special?

a) _____

b) _____

Daily affirmation: I am . . .

_____

_____

Amazing things that happened today:

a) _____

b) _____

I could have made this day even better if I had . . .

_____

_____

End your day with a blessing:

_____

_____

Day 50

Date: ___/___/20___

As we look ahead into the next century,
leaders will be those who empower others.

Bill Gates

I am grateful for . . .

a) _____

b) _____

What would make my day special?

a) _____

b) _____

Daily affirmation: I am . . .

_____

_____

Amazing things that happened today:

a) _____

b) _____

I could have made this day even better if I had . . .

_____

_____

End your day with a blessing:

_____

_____

Day 51

Date: ___/___/20___

Sufferings end when you *choose* not to suffer.
Chaitali Mehta

I am grateful for . . .

a) _____

b) _____

What would make my day special?

a) _____

b) _____

Daily affirmation: I am . . .

_____

_____

Amazing things that happened today:

a) _____

b) _____

I could have made this day even better if I had . . .

_____

_____

End your day with a blessing:

_____

_____

Day 52

Date: ____/____/20____

You get in life what you have the courage to ask for.
Oprah Winfrey

I am grateful for . . .

a) _____

b) _____

What would make my day special?

a) _____

b) _____

Daily affirmation: I am . . .

_____

_____

Amazing things that happened today:

a) _____

b) _____

I could have made this day even better if I had . . .

_____

_____

End your day with a blessing:

_____

_____

Day 53

Date: ___/___/20___

Don't work for happiness, work happily.

Anonymous

I am grateful for . . .

a) _____

b) _____

What would make my day special?

a) _____

b) _____

Daily affirmation: I am . . .

_____

_____

Amazing things that happened today:

a) _____

b) _____

I could have made this day even better if I had . . .

_____

_____

End your day with a blessing:

_____

_____

Day 54

Date: ____/____/20____

HOPE means Hold On, Pain Ends.

Anonymous

I am grateful for . . .

a) _____

b) _____

What would make my day special?

a) _____

b) _____

Daily affirmation: I am . . .

_____

_____

Amazing things that happened today:

a) _____

b) _____

I could have made this day even better if I had . . .

_____

_____

End your day with a blessing:

_____

_____

Weekly Challenge

(Go to the list of weekly challenges on page no. 141,
pick any one of the challenges, and go for it!)

Day 55

Date: ___/___/20___

You can't cross the sea merely by
standing and staring at the water.

Rabindranath Tagore

I am grateful for . . .

a) _____

b) _____

What would make my day special?

a) _____

b) _____

Daily affirmation: I am . . .

_____

_____

Amazing things that happened today:

a) _____

b) _____

I could have made this day even better if I had . . .

_____

_____

End your day with a blessing:

_____

_____

Day 56

Date: ____/____/20____

I will not let anyone walk through
my mind with their dirty feet.
Mahatma Gandhi

I am grateful for . . .

a) _____

b) _____

What would make my day special?

a) _____

b) _____

Daily affirmation: I am . . .

_____

_____

Amazing things that happened today:

a) _____

b) _____

I could have made this day even better if I had . . .

_____

_____

End your day with a blessing:

_____

_____

Day 57

Date: ___/___/20___

Nobody can hurt me without my permission.
Mahatma Gandhi

I am grateful for . . .

a) _____

b) _____

What would make my day special?

a) _____

b) _____

Daily affirmation: I am . . .

_____

_____

Amazing things that happened today:

a) _____

b) _____

I could have made this day even better if I had . . .

_____

_____

End your day with a blessing:

_____

_____

Day 58

Date: ___/___/20___

I don't want to be liked. I want to be respected.

Jack Ma

I am grateful for . . .

a) _____

b) _____

What would make my day special?

a) _____

b) _____

Daily affirmation: I am . . .

_____

_____

Amazing things that happened today:

a) _____

b) _____

I could have made this day even better if I had . . .

_____

_____

End your day with a blessing:

_____

_____

Day 59

Date: ___/___/20___

Don't compare yourself to anyone in this world . . .
If you do so, you are insulting yourself.

Bill Gates

I am grateful for . . .

a) _____

b) _____

What would make my day special?

a) _____

b) _____

Daily affirmation: I am . . .

_____

_____

Amazing things that happened today:

a) _____

b) _____

I could have made this day even better if I had . . .

_____

_____

End your day with a blessing:

_____

_____

Day 60

Date: ___/___/20___

Have the courage to follow your
heart and intuition.

Steve Jobs

I am grateful for . . .

a) _____

b) _____

What would make my day special?

a) _____

b) _____

Daily affirmation: I am . . .

_____

_____

Amazing things that happened today:

a) _____

b) _____

I could have made this day even better if I had . . .

_____

_____

End your day with a blessing:

_____

_____

Day 61

Date: ___/___/20___

The purpose of your life is to find your purpose
and give your whole heart and soul to it.

Buddha

I am grateful for . . .

a) _____

b) _____

What would make my day special?

a) _____

b) _____

Daily affirmation: I am . . .

_____

_____

Amazing things that happened today:

a) _____

b) _____

I could have made this day even better if I had . . .

_____

_____

End your day with a blessing:

_____

_____

Weekly Challenge

(Go to the list of weekly challenges on page no. 141,
pick any one of the challenges, and go for it!)

Day 62

Date: ___/___/20___

Give the ones you love — wings to fly,
roots to come back and reasons to stay.

Dalai Lama

I am grateful for . . .

a) _____
b) _____

What would make my day special?

a) _____
b) _____

Daily affirmation: I am . . .

_____

_____

Amazing things that happened today:

a) _____
b) _____

I could have made this day even better if I had . . .

_____

_____

End your day with a blessing:

_____

_____

Day 63

Date: ___/___/20___

Health is the greatest gift, contentment the
greatest wealth, faithfulness the best relationship.

Buddha

I am grateful for . . .

a) _____

b) _____

What would make my day special?

a) _____

b) _____

Daily affirmation: I am . . .

_____

_____

Amazing things that happened today:

a) _____

b) _____

I could have made this day even better if I had . . .

_____

_____

End your day with a blessing:

_____

_____

Today is a special day in your life. You have completed three cycles
of twenty-one days of writing in this amazing diary and filling

it with all your dreams and emotions. Now you have deepened your convictions, and you have started attracting all your success. You need to order your next diary to continue defining and refining your life.

Day 64

Date: ___/___/20___

Heroes are not made in the battlefield. They
are created in the cradle by nurturing hands.

Chaitali Mehta

I am grateful for . . .

a) _____

b) _____

What would make my day special?

a) _____

b) _____

Daily affirmation: I am . . .

_____

_____

Amazing things that happened today:

a) _____

b) _____

I could have made this day even better if I had . . .

_____

_____

End your day with a blessing:

_____

_____

Day 65

Date: ____/____/20____

A dream is not the thing you see in your sleep;
it is that thing that doesn't let you sleep.
                              Dr APJ Abdul Kalam

I am grateful for . . .

a) _____

b) _____

What would make my day special?

a) _____

b) _____

Daily affirmation: I am . . .

_____

_____

Amazing things that happened today:

a) _____

b) _____

I could have made this day even better if I had . . .

_____

_____

End your day with a blessing:

_____

_____

Day 66

Date: ____/____/20____

You don't have to attain salvation; you need to
live life with full and complete awareness.

Morari Bapu

I am grateful for . . .

a) _____

b) _____

What would make my day special?

a) _____

b) _____

Daily affirmation: I am . . .

_____

_____

Amazing things that happened today:

a) _____

b) _____

I could have made this day even better if I had . . .

_____

_____

End your day with a blessing:

_____

_____

Day 67

Date: ___/___/20___

Everybody wants success but *success* wants—
determination, dedication, devotion and discipline.
Chaitali Mehta

I am grateful for . . .

a) _____

b) _____

What would make my day special?

a) _____

b) _____

Daily affirmation: I am . . .

_____

_____

Amazing things that happened today:

a) _____

b) _____

I could have made this day even better if I had . . .

_____

_____

End your day with a blessing:

_____

_____

Weekly Challenge

(Go to the list of weekly challenges on page no. 141,
pick any one of the challenges, and go for it!)

Day 68

Date: ___/___/20___

You cannot shake hands with a clenched fist.
                              Indira Gandhi

I am grateful for . . .

a) _____

b) _____

What would make my day special?

a) _____

b) _____

Daily affirmation: I am . . .

_____

_____

Amazing things that happened today:

a) _____

b) _____

I could have made this day even better if I had . . .

_____

_____

End your day with a blessing:

_____

_____

Day 69

Date: ___/___/20___

What doesn't kill you, makes you stronger!

MS Dhoni

I am grateful for . . .

a) _____

b) _____

What would make my day special?

a) _____

b) _____

Daily affirmation: I am . . .

_____

_____

Amazing things that happened today:

a) _____

b) _____

I could have made this day even better if I had . . .

_____

_____

End your day with a blessing:

_____

_____

Day 70

Date: ___/___/20___

When the whole world is silent, even
one voice becomes powerful.

Malala Yousafzai

I am grateful for . . .

a) _____

b) _____

What would make my day special?

a) _____

b) _____

Daily affirmation: I am . . .

_____

_____

Amazing things that happened today:

a) _____

b) _____

I could have made this day even better if I had . . .

_____

_____

End your day with a blessing:

_____

_____

Day 71

Date: ____/____/20____

Take risks in your life.
If you win; you may lead.
If you lose; you may guide.
Swami Vivekananda

I am grateful for . . .

a) _____

b) _____

What would make my day special?

a) _____

b) _____

Daily affirmation: I am . . .

_____

_____

Amazing things that happened today:

a) _____

b) _____

I could have made this day even better if I had . . .

_____

_____

End your day with a blessing:

_____

_____

Weekly Challenge

(Go to the list of weekly challenges on page no. 141,
pick any one of the challenges, and go for it!)

Day 72

Date: ___/___/20___

It always seems impossible until it's done.
Nelson Mandela

I am grateful for . . .

a) _____

b) _____

What would make my day special?

a) _____

b) _____

Daily affirmation: I am . . .

_____

_____

Amazing things that happened today:

a) _____

b) _____

I could have made this day even better if I had . . .

_____

_____

End your day with a blessing:

_____

_____

Hello, my friend!

You have completed ten weeks of writing in your diary. I am sure now that this diary is among the best of your friends.

The team that has collectively contributed to creating this book is grateful to you for having faith and belief in our vision that *anyone can become successful in life if he has the right attitude and a burning desire for it.*

We would love to hear from you about your experiences in developing the habit of writing in this diary. Please share with us your valuable feedback.

How has this diary helped you in defining and refining your life? Email us at definetorefineyourlife@gmail.com

We hope you have a new copy of your diary so you can continue writing tomorrow.

WEEKLY CHALLENGE
Time for myself, my life, my actions

Choose any one challenge each week and go for it!

1. Get rid of one item that does not make you happy.
2. Go for a walk today and listen to your favourite music.
3. Ask a co-worker, friend, or client out for lunch this week.
4. Go and attend a musical concert (old songs).
5. Watch your favourite comedy movie/cartoon/Charlie Chaplin movie.
6. Switch off your mobile for two hours and enjoy some "Me" time.
7. Compliment a stranger today.
8. Look into the mirror and say *'I love you, you are the best'.*
9. Visit a place of worship and sit quietly for some time.
10. Donate some money for a social cause.
11. Go shopping and buy something for yourself.
12. Eat your favourite food, like chocolate or ice cream, and enjoy it.
13. Meditate. Close your eyes, feel the cosmos within you, ask anything of the universe, and wait for the answer in silence and belief.
14. Try a new cuisine or beverage.
15. Take some chocolates to your workplace and distribute.
16. Visit an orphanage and gift some goodies.
17. Plant trees in a nearby garden or have a potted plant in your house.
18. Sleep under the sky and feel the vastness of this universe.
19. Go to your old school, meet your teachers, and cherish old memories.
20. Go to a stadium to watch a match.
21. Play board games like Scrabble, Ludo, or Chess with your parents.
22. Sing your favourite songs or play a musical instrument.
23. Have a pet? Spend some time with it.
24. Invite your friends over for a night out at your place and have fun.
25. Review your diary today and see the miracles that have happened in your life.

26. Plan a picnic with your near and dear ones.
27. Go cycling, enjoy badminton or table tennis, or simply solve puzzles or crosswords... or sudoku, if you like!
28. Play a prank on your friends or siblings.
29. Plan a surprise for your grandparents.
30. Get a new haircut or go in for a makeover.
31. Have a full-body check-up.
32. Arrange your wardrobe, study table, workplace, or kitchen.
33. Go to the terrace and watch the sun rise.
34. Go through some old photographs and enjoy.
35. Visit a new religious place, other than the places of your religion.
36. Donate books or clothes to the needy.
37. Have a candlelight dinner at home.
38. Forgive at least one person in your life and write in this diary: '[Name], I forgive you from the deepest corner of my heart, and I hereby pray to God to help both of us in this process of healing.'
39. Give a paid leave to your servant voluntarily.
40. Make a bucket list of all the crazy ideas you would like to do or places you wish to travel to.
41. Travel by an unreserved compartment to your village.
42. Catch a stand-up comedy show... Live!
43. Participate in a marathon organised in your city or town.
44. Go to flag-hoisting events on Republic Day and Independence Day.
45. Plan to visit New Delhi on Republic Day to watch the parade at least once in your lifetime with your loved ones.

DAILY AFFIRMATIONS

Daily affirmations have the power to reinstate, refresh, and help us redefine our vision and goals in life. You may choose from the list whichever you wish to attract in your life, but it is advisable to write your own affirmations, which will include your strong emotions and convictions. You can write in your mother tongue, which your mind can easily connect to.

General Affirmations

1. I am the best.
2. I am a winner.
3. I have a winning attitude.
4. Today is my day.
5. God is with me.
6. I am divinely guided by the Almighty.
7. I can do it.
8. I am always enthusiastic and energetic in whatever work I do.
9. I listen, I decide, I focus, and I implement.
10. I love what I do; I do what I love.
11. I grow when I help others grow.
12. I give what I want.
13. I follow my heart.
14. I have the immense capacity to do what I desire.
15. I am like a proton, always positive.
16. I lead a healthy, wealthy, and happy life.
17. I respect my health, my wealth, and my happiness.
18. I deserve nothing but the best and the finest.
19. Integrity and honesty is my way of life.
20. I spread and experience love wherever I go.
21. All is well in my world.
22. I choose to accept myself completely with love.
23. I am in complete harmony with this universe.
24. The universe conspires to fulfil all my wishes.

25. I am enjoying every moment of my life.
26. I am always positive, prosperous, and progressive in my life.

Affirmations to Attract Money and Prosperity

27. I attract money, well-being, healthy relationships, and happiness.
28. I am a money magnet.
29. My work gives me immense pleasure, refreshes my mind, and gives solace to my soul.
30. I am attracting abundant money in my life.
31. I earn money effortlessly.
32. Wealth is constantly flowing into my life.
33. Money is an important part of my life.
34. I am enjoying the money I have.
35. Money is my constant companion.
36. Money leads me to growth and prosperity.

Affirmations to Attract Excellent Health

37. Day by day, in every way, I am becoming better and better.
38. I am fit and fine.
39. Every cell of my body is radiating health, happiness, and harmony.
40. My body is functioning in complete harmony.
41. I love my body.
42. I have developed a healthy eating habit.
43. I can sleep peacefully, and I am at ease.
44. My body and mind are in harmony.
45. I am full of energy and strength.
46. Everything I eat or drink heals me.

Affirmations for Students

47. I am a winner; I love achieving my goals.
48. I am always in a receptive mood.
49. I happily receive knowledge.

50. My ability to learn and remember is increasing day by day.
51. I am surrounded by friends who inspire and motivate me to grow in life.
52. I am a quick learner.
53. I am a champion.
54. I am always open to knowledge and learning.
55. I am grateful to my teachers, who give me knowledge.
56. I always get excellent grades.

Affirmations for Success

57. There are infinite possibilities and opportunities for me.
58. Success is the by-product of fulfilling every commitment I make to myself.
59. I am always in the company of positive, energetic, and dynamic people.
60. Whatever I decide is RIGHT for me.
61. I decide what is right for me!
62. I am running a successful business.
63. My business helps contribute to the world.
64. My investments give me multifold returns.
65. I work when I want, where I want, and with the people I want to work with.
66. Positive and dynamic people connect with me and help my business prosper.
67. I am always at the right place at the right time with the right people.
68. My work is my worship.
69. I am able to achieve any goal I set for my business.
70. I easily and happily attract my clients.

Affirmations for Healthy Relationships

71. I give love and get love.
72. I have a positive and loving attitude.

73. I am always surrounded by loving, caring, and compassionate people.
74. My life is a celebration.
75. I enjoy love and warmth in every relationship.
76. I can easily connect with people around me with love and positivity.
77. I enjoy a strong bond with each member of my family.
78. My relationships are incredible.
79. I nurture my relationships with love, care, trust, and support.
80. I enjoy honest relationships.
81. I attract happy and long-lasting relationships.